The Mother Of Transformation

How to create a family first
freedom led life with love

To Emily, Xavier & Caspar

Contents

Welcome and thank you for being here,

I'm Gayle Berry and I've created this offering to help you fully step into your power as a mother and welcome the magic of reinvention into your life. This is transformational work; I know because I've lived it. In this book, I'm sharing my own experiences and the personal transformations I've been through during the last twenty-plus years. As well as reminding you of your incredible power as a mother, I want to inspire you to ignite your passion and purpose by listening to your heart and being true to yourself. This is how I live. This is how I work. It is what I feel and believe.

I want to acknowledge that I am writing from a place of being a white woman, with access to privilege and many aspects of life that other mothers do not have, such as health care and education. Everyone's journey is different, and we all start from a different place due to social injustice and it is important to acknowledge this.

The most important principle to remember in this book is that everything changes. Growth is life. When we are able to find true balance and harmony with ourselves and others, we get to live a rich and joyful life; a life where we all support and care for each other. Embracing it all - life and death, light and shadow, expansion and contraction - is all part of the flow of existence, and you are not separate from it. Remember what I said at the beginning, everything changes. We are in a constant state of flow. When you trust that your path is waiting for you, it's easier to take the first step to being more of you, and not less, and to embrace the beauty of reinvention. I believe in the power of intention and vision, I believe this rests inside us all, and that it manifests in different ways for each of us.

My story - The many reinventions of Gayle Berry.

We reinvent ourselves every day; sometimes consciously, often unconsciously. I wanted to share a few of my more transformational reinventions so far, so you can understand why I am sharing my experiences and wisdom with you.

Motherhood

The first and most significant reinvention for me was becoming a mother and was the greatest transformation ever. When I became a mother for the first time with my daughter, Emily, my whole life changed. I finally understood what unconditional love really was. I knew my passion and purpose on this earth was now to support Emily in her journey. I understood the power of nurturing love in a way I never imagined, and I just wanted to be with her and put my family first in all I did. This was the most unexpected experience for me as I had never thought about becoming a mother. I'd never been overly interested in babies before and had never held a baby until the moment Emily was placed in my arms. It was in that moment that I left my old identity behind and embraced a new, beautiful phase of my life. At the time, I didn't have any friends who'd had babies. My family was very small, I had no cousins growing up, so it came as a bit of a shock to me that when I became pregnant, having my own baby resonated so deeply in my body. This was what I had been waiting for my whole life: the opportunity to be a mother, to mother another, and to heal any wounds that were traveling through my ancestral line around mothering, creating a new path of connected love through my family. This was my first rebirth.

Entrepreneurship

The second reinvention came from starting Blossom & Berry. I reinvented myself from a corporate finance lawyer working in the city to an entrepreneur. I had no idea how to do this, no time, no money, and with three children under three and a half. I knew that freedom, love, connection, and creativity were my four highest values, and that entrepreneurship would be the way that I'd be able to activate that in the world. So, despite many comments from those around me that this maybe wasn't the most sensible thing to do, I took the bold step to jump from my corporate career into becoming an entrepreneur and starting my own local business. Over the last twenty years, I have grown that local business (that started with two mums and babies in my front room), into a multiple six-figure global family with over 2000 teachers, five global branches, numerous charitable projects, different product ranges, books, events, retreats, and so much more that is beyond my wildest dreams. My business has brought me the most beautiful gifts that I could ever receive. Blossom & Berry grew through trusting the process and believing that anything is possible. I believe entrepreneurship is a force for good and helps to serve the world through creativity and transformation. When you share your gifts to relieve pain and suffering and bring joy and happiness to the world through transformation, that is service. Being in the deepest service to parents and babies is what I was born to do. I truly believe this as it feels effortless and easy to me. In the more than twenty years that I've been growing Blossom & Berry, I've never had burnout, I've never had points where I felt stagnant, and I've never wanted to give up. Yes, I've had huge challenges, massive lessons, things come into my path that have slowed me down, and ultimately, if I am honest, my marriage ended because of my passion and purpose, but over the years I have had the resilience to keep going because I believe in the power of love. I know that I'm here to teach love to parents and babies around the world. I know I'm here to create connected community and to contribute to the world in this beautiful way because I believe that love creates love. I know that when I love, support, and nurture my teachers, they love support and nurture parents and carers who in turn love, support, and nurture their babies. Those babies get to grow-up knowing they are fully loved, seen, heard, and accepted, and they go out into the world and interact with others with love. This is how we change the world, one baby at a time. This is how we nurture the future. This is what is absolutely central to my passion and purpose here on earth.

Philanthropy

My third reinvention was when I decided to set up my charitable project in Malawi, empowering mothers to learn how to become infant massage instructors and learn about menstrual hygiene, early childhood development, and kangaroo care. I set up a programme called the Mother and Infant Health Initiative that allowed women to become community leaders and hold space for other Malawian women to learn about infant mental health. Ten years ago, I went to Malawi to train staff who were supporting the most vulnerable babies in baby orphanages the benefits of nurturing touch. I meant to go on one trip only, when I was forty. What actually happened was I fell in love with Malawi, the hearts of the people I met, and with the two founders of Love Support Unite, Nina and Alice, who had helped me make the connections.

After that first trip, I was invited to develop my project to reach more babies in need, so I became a co-founder of the charity. For the last ten years I have been providing training, training bursaries, and financial support for Early Childhood Development projects. In addition to this, we built a nursery, supported babies with additional needs, and have hosted trainings for nursery staff in Malawi to learn from volunteers from the UK, and vice versa.

This stage of my life was unexpected and a huge reinvention because I only meant to go to Malawi for a single visit. The impact it has had on my life is something I never could have seen coming. It started by getting on a plane to Malawi after buying some magic sunglasses, called Love Specs, at a festival created by Love Support Unite, and ended up with building a nursery for children, volunteer trips, and fundraising. I went on to become the UK Director of Love Support Unite, helping to raise over one-hundred-thousand pounds with the team, and I received the Points of Light Award from Downing Street for my contribution towards this. I also received the most amazing, magical friends and experiences from being in Malawi. I'm forever grateful for that experience; it changed me deeply as a person. I realised my own privilege in this world, and it made me want to be an advocate for human rights and social justice.

Loving Millions

The fourth big reinvention I had was becoming a global business mentor. I felt that I had so much experience after over twenty years in business and philanthropy, that now was the time to become a business mentor.

I set up the Love Millions Academy because I wanted to love and impact millions of people by helping other leaders' step into their love, leadership, and ability to create a legacy. I believe that we are here to impact millions, receive millions, and to contribute millions, because as we receive, we give. This is the cycle of life. As entrepreneurs leading with love, we have an opportunity to redirect the flow of energy and money into conscious projects, communities, and businesses around the world that create community and transformation. This really excites me. Through my mentoring business, I've been able to work with incredible clients and elevate their businesses, add value, and help grow their communities. I've also been able to travel the world creating beautiful retreats and collaborating with amazing people. I believe we can help each other by activating our gifts and exchanging our valuable energy. Conscious entrepreneurship and love activism allows us to embed the values of equity, togetherness, and shared power. You are the change the world is looking for.

Reverence for Nature

The next chapter of my life, and my current reinvention, is working much more in alignment with nature, looking at the path of shamanism, and looking at how to protect this beautiful planet that we live on by being an advocate for climate justice, looking at other inequalities in the world, and doing my best to try to help others from my place of privilege. Responsible travel and adventure is on the cards, as well as connecting with other beautiful souls around the world.

I hope this book inspires you to know that anything is possible when you decide to become the person you know you are inside. You are the song waiting to be written, and the world is here to receive your music.

Let's begin...

As I shared, I made the mother of all reinventions by leaving my job as a corporate finance lawyer in the city with amazing prospects - and after spending seven years studying law and doing various other postgraduate courses to become a lawyer - and deciding to teach baby massage after the birth of my beautiful daughter, Emily. I had to completely abandon my comfortable identity to step into the unknown, doing something that was completely and utterly foreign to me, which was becoming an entrepreneur, running my own business, facilitating groups, and supporting parents and babies. I made that jump by trusting and tuning into my heart.

As a result of this giant leap of faith twenty-two years ago, I have received a life beyond my wildest dreams. And I don't say that lightly. I say it with humility and gratitude, because I have been able to spend incredible time with my family as they've been growing up, including all those tiny moments when they were babies, to school holidays, trips and plays, prom nights, and travel adventures. I'm so glad I was there for it all. Those times made me the person that I am today and made my three beautiful children the people that they are, giving me the greatest gift in my life: the most amazing relationship with my children.

All of this came from trusting my heart, trusting the process, and making that leap to reinvent myself, to become the person I desired to be, to create the lifestyle for myself and my family I wanted, and to live in a state of magic and awe knowing that anything is possible.

So, this transmission is to give you the confidence and the permission (not that you need my permission, because you have everything inside of you to do whatever it is that you desire), to reinvent yourself at this incredible moment in time where you have transitioned from maiden to mother. You have experienced the energetic shift that occurs, as a result of becoming pregnant and carrying and creating a new life within your body; something that is not celebrated enough for the absolute sacred act that it is. Your body has brought forth another human being. Your incredible body is a portal for magic. That is the power that you hold within yourself when you become a mother. If you can create and grow and give birth to a human being, you can do anything. That is your power.

Unfortunately, in many parts of the world, in many societies, in many cultures, this act of incredible power and magic is not celebrated. It is not acknowledged, it is not valued, it is just seen as something that happens and then we are expected to get on with the day-to-day existence of juggling all of the things, along with all of the ideas that are given to us about what 'mothering' is and what a mother should be doing. In fact, you are incredible, and that power that you have tapped into is the power that can create anything in your life. I really want you to repeat this mantra: "If I can create a human being with my body, I can create anything I desire. I can manifest anything in my life. I can grow anything in my life". Just like your baby grew from the dark space of your womb, anything that is currently in your imagination but is not yet manifested into reality, can be birthed.

Anything that exists in that space of nothing has the ability to become everything, and you have the ability to create whatever it is that you desire: the lifestyle that you desire, the vibration of your life that you desire, the people, places, things that you desire. The evidence that you have created a human is all you need to know.

We can see this in nature and when we look at Mother Earth. You put a seed into the ground and from that seed come roots and shoots and branches and leaves, and then fruit that we eat, which nourishes us. Mother Earth is abundant in all ways because she is creating life. You are abundant in all ways because you have created life. The same ability Mother Earth has to create abundance is the same ability that you have to create abundance. We have just forgotten.

Go outside and see yourself reflected in nature. See what's coming out of the ground all of the time, because the power that supports that is the same power that you have within you. You have the power to create. You have the power to reinvent. You have the power to clear and kill any old versions of you that are no longer in alignment with the type of lifestyle that you desire to be in, right here, right now. In reality, all old versions of you have gone and do not exist. That version of you only exists in your mind, as a result of the beliefs that you hold about yourself. So, once you decide that you want to reinvent yourself, once you decide you want to be reborn, once you decide that it is time for the caterpillar to go into the cocoon and emerge as the butterfly, it happens.

Maybe it's already started to happen which is why you are reading this book now. Maybe you've already felt parts of you changing or you've lost parts of yourself in this process of becoming a mother. It's really important to grieve those parts, to honour them and not dismiss that it is a difficult process to let go of your identity and all that you have known, so that you can become the butterfly. The old identity that you were holding as maiden may have been comfortable, and your friends, your lifestyle, all of those things were comfortable. Now as a mother with your baby, things are unknown.

There are some powerful principles to ground you and these are the ones I have used myself, so I can vouch for the fact they work and can offer you so much. I would love to share these with you.

They are:

Acceptance

Gratitude

Vision

Planning

Action

This book will cover them all and invite you to co-create from a place of awareness.

Contemplation One - Acceptance

The first process in transformation is accepting that the old version of you no longer exists. It is in this moment, right now, that you have the power to create what it is that you desire, to reinvent yourself, to create the life that you desire with your family, with your baby, with your child. It doesn't matter how you were parented and what effect this has had on your life. We all have trauma, wounds, stories or limiting beliefs from our own experiences but you get to change that path here and now, with your own family. You get to clear it, to break any intergenerational bonds or chains of trauma. You get to clear your ancestral line by deciding here and now that 'I am a sovereign being, and I am going to choose to reinvent myself, to reinvent the way I'm going to be with my family, to reinvent my ancestral line. I'm going to be an amazing ancestor for all of the future members of my family because it starts with me.'

When you accept that the old versions of you are gone and no longer here, that means that you start afresh and create a soil that is ripe for you to plant in. That's when it gets really exciting.

When I was a lawyer working in the city, I did not like it, it was not aligned with me and I was miserable.

I had social anxiety, I had a blushing complex, I was stuck big time. I actually got down on my hands and knees when I was traveling in Peru, between finishing my training contract as a lawyer and starting my job, and I said: 'Please, please help me. Please show me the way, because I don't know the way to go and I'm so miserable and I'm so unhappy, and I just don't know what to do.' Within two weeks I was pregnant with my daughter, Emily. She was a happy accident. It was very unplanned and my whole life changed from that moment. That's when my reinvention started, because at that moment I became the guardian of my daughter. I had a new life growing inside of me. I was just in love from that moment, and I travelled through my pregnancy with this deep desire to meet my daughter, not knowing what that meant, having never held a baby in my life. Yet I knew that this was going to mean a new life for me, a rebirth, a reinvention of myself. And when my daughter was given to me after a very long labour, I couldn't believe that I had my precious little girl in my arms. I was in love with everything.

I realised that she was the greatest gift that I would ever receive in my life. From that moment I was going to dedicate myself to being her guide, her teacher. I wanted to spend the most amount of time I possibly could with her because I knew that she was going to teach me about love. This was my chance to create a new story for my family and to parent in a different way. I was also going to get to be a child again, to embrace the process of revisiting the world as a place full of magic, wonder and awe. I approached parenting with an open heart and through co-creating a path with Emily, knowing that my ultimate goal was to spend the most amount of time with her, to be present with her, to be connected with her, because that's what mattered to me most.

Even though I had no experience of babies at all, and I was working in the city in a very masculine environment, when I had Emily, that's when the reinvention started. I stepped into my feminine power. I decided that I was going to accept that being a mother was going to have ups and downs, challenges, and celebrations. It wasn't going be a linear path, it was going to be full of magic and mystery. I accepted that there would be moments of feeling out of control and moments when I would feel more at home than ever before. I surrendered to the fact that the journey of the mother was going to be different to that of the maiden. The journey of the mother is, for me, defined by love, nurturing, care and connection, and by presence and time, because the journey of the mother is about relationship.

I believe that your children come into your life to show you where you can heal, to show you where maybe your darker spots are, where your wounds are. Through the relationship with your children you can reinvent yourself, you can heal yourself because those triggers are shown to you. We have a choice to embrace them, to heal them, and to transcend them and to be more love. It is such a beautiful process.

I very quickly had three children in three and a half years. I had my two sons in close succession; I was pregnant with my third son Caspar when my middle son, Xavier, was only seven months old. And again, I learned that this was about acceptance. There was a reason why I became pregnant so quickly. It wasn't planned, it was a happy accident, again! Three children under three and a half could have seemed overwhelming, however that is where I found myself. It was a beautiful gift. You know, not everyone gets to have children. Not everyone gets to have a second child or third child. I went from having my daughter to having a family fast. It was deep acceptance and deep surrender and letting go again of ideas and timelines and attachments to how those had to be, that allowed flow. I let go of any expectation of myself. I let go of comparing myself to what anybody else would be doing. I focused solely on creating a life that was in alignment with my highest values, which are joy, magic, wonder, awe, love, connection, and flow, over and above anything else. I was able to reinvent myself by trusting in these higher values and trusting in the path, even though I couldn't see the way.

By trusting and aligning myself to those values and their vibrations, even when things were tough and we had no money, were overdrawn on our overdraft, didn't go on holiday for many years (and when we did we were camping in a tent on the Isle of Wight with three kids under nine with howling wind and no money), I had gratitude in my heart for the fact that this was freedom to me, freedom to BE me. In the reinvention process, that's when you get to remember who you really are. The more that you are you, the more that you are the essence of who you are, the more you are the truest, fullest expression of who you are, the less energy you will have to spend being anything other than that and the more energy you will have for the things you love in your life.

The people, places, things that you attract into your life will be in alignment with your true essence, which makes your relationships so much easier and flow better. This all comes from being brave enough to reinvent yourself and remember who you are. Let go of the masks, the stories, the beliefs, and all of the things that have been holding together this old identity of yours. Reinvention is the natural state of flow. We are reinventing ourselves in every single moment, in every single minute, in every single day. The moment we wake up in the morning, the old version of us from yesterday has gone. Once we start to realise that the process of life is a process of reinvention, reinventing yourself by making gigantic leaps from one thing to the other, like leaving a nine to five, to creating a life that's in alignment, doesn't feel so scary because actually it's the natural process of life.

If we try to resist change and we try to resist reinvention, then we can become stagnant and we may not reach our potential and bear our fruit, or receive the abundance available to us, because we're in this stagnant energy. When there is acceptance of where you are, acceptance that life is a process, acceptance that everything changes, acceptance, that nothing ever stays the same, acceptance that you are where you are, and that this is another beautiful day of your life that you get to live, then things begin to flow and magic happens. Some people didn't get to wake up today, they weren't on the wake-up list, but you were, so take radical responsibility for your life.

What has gone has gone. Maybe you need to throw a kind of grief party, to say goodbye to those things that have served you up until this point, that you are really grateful for. Now you are accepting that those parts of you are not travelling with you into the future. Let go of relationships, habits, behaviours, jobs, food, anything in your life that is no longer in alignment with the future version of you and no longer in alignment with your values. It's so powerful to accept your power as a creator and to accept that you have the ability to take radical responsibility for your life and to choose what you want. You can reflect on the idea that everything that has occurred in your life has been the result of your choice. Whether you are conscious of it or not, we are manifesting all of the time with our thoughts, with our perceptions, with our beliefs.

This is the pivotal moment, where you get to choose to reinvent yourself in whatever way is the most nourishing and nurturing for this part of your life.

So, what do you need to accept about your life now?

I am in control, I will always be OK + life is happen for me.

What do you need to let go of? What do you need to forgive, whether it's other people or yourself?

The fear that others will hurt me, forgive myself for all the anxiety I cause myself to stay safe.

What do you need to notice?

That I can let the anxiety go now and allow myself to enjoy the present, more fun + ja

What do you need to bring into your awareness today, so that you can make choices about the future that are in alignment with what it is that you desire?

Belief in my dreams feel worthy of that life and take action to make it happen.

Pick up a journal and start to dream.

Let go of what doesn't work.

24

Contemplation Two - Gratitude.

The vibration of gratitude is one of the most powerful vibrations that exists because when we are grateful for what we have, we feel abundant. When we feel abundant, the vibration that we are holding is abundance; so we attract more abundance to us when we are aware of what it is that we are already receiving every single day.

Now, you might not at the moment be receiving exactly what it is that you want (or what your ego mind wants), or what you see around you that you think you should want or what looks like success, material safety, or like you've 'made it'. In actual fact, you are always receiving. In every single moment you are receiving; you are receiving effortlessly through your breath right now. We just take for granted that the trees outside are making the oxygen that allows us to breathe.

Without the trees, we wouldn't be able to breathe. So, there's a whole lot of gratitude for you to feel, for nature, for the trees. Now you will never walk past a tree again without thinking, 'Wow, because of you I can breathe. Thank you!' That's gratitude. When you look at the earth and you think that the earth is creating food for you to eat, that's gratitude. When you really connect with the fact that you can put seeds in the earth and incredible juicy fruit and crops come out of the ground for us to eat so that we can be nourished and nurtured, that is gratitude. We are surrounded by beautiful animals and nature. We get sunshine every day. We get rain. We have water and fire. We have everything provided for us every single day, abundantly with no conditions. It just happens. We are constantly receiving. We are in a state of receptivity at all times.

Just the fact that we are alive, we are receiving, and that we get to be here is incredible. It's a miracle that you're even here in the first place; that is enough to start to cultivate a deep sense of gratitude. Then we can remember that as humans, we are powerful creators. We have desires, we have intentions, and it's the process of creation that expands the universe. For example, if you are a poet and you want to write a poem, and that's your desire and your intention, when you create that poem there is something new and beautiful that has been added into the world that is for the enjoyment of everybody. Your poem then goes on to inspire someone else to write a poem, and their poem inspires somebody else, and so on. These poems are read at births, marriages and funerals, in celebration, and to create togetherness. For me this is how the universe, all the creative ideas in the universe and all of the amazing love in the world, is created through the individual expression of every single person's heart that adds to the beautiful mix, the interconnected web of love and creativity. It's incredible. Having intentions and desires is amazing and a gift to the world. When we are able to tune into the gratitude, the wonder, the beauty, and the awe of life, this vibration powers up the creativity inside of you that then allows you to set the intention to personally express more of yourself in life. It's like another little flower on the unconnected tree of life is born through you. That flower bears fruit that then feeds us all.

We are all in this beautiful, abundant, interconnected web of life. It's just so beautiful when you start to think about life like that. Every single person is adding to this abundant life. That starts when you reinvent yourself or remember who you are and start to honour your personal expression. So regardless of what you've done up until this moment, now you get to choose who you are. Sometimes when we are mothers, we think, well how I am going to do that? I haven't got any space to do that. I'm caring for my baby or my child. Unless you choose to authentically express yourself, unless you choose to honour who you are, you are setting yourself up for a lifelong relationship with your child - the person that you probably are going be loving the most, and definitely the person who is going to look to you the most - and you are not going to be authentic. The amount of energy you're going to have to spend being somebody that you are not is going to be huge if you start pretending now. You can stop all that here and now and make a commitment to yourself that you must be yourself. Now is the moment to be 100% you and to invite your baby into that world with you. You don't have to let go of who you are in your essence, instead you honour who you truly are and get to fully express that version of you.

This is big stuff and that can feel scary, but your baby is watching you and you can't hide from those eyes. Babies are very clever because they come down to this planet as 100% love and when you're in the presence of someone who is 100% love, they do not hide their emotions. They express their needs. They are there right in front of you in the vibration of being 100% love. Babies don't have thoughts or judgements about themselves. They're simply there. They are like the clearest mirror that you could possibly ever have reflecting back everything at you. All of the things about you that are difficult, that might be hard for you to hold, that might be making you feel uncomfortable, your baby will show you. Babies make us look at ourselves. They are our greatest teachers. They are our greatest healers. When babies show us where we need to grow, we have to decide:

'Am I going to push these feelings away, or am I going to sit with them and work them out? What's going on here? Am I going to be something that I'm not? Am I going to create an identity that doesn't sit with me, but pleases others? Am I going to worry and stress about everything? Or am I just going to relax and say hey, I don't really know what's going on here. This is the magic and mystery of life. Baby do you want to kind of co-create with me? Shall we do this journey together? Shall we trust each other? Shall we communicate with each other? Shall we spend time with each other to get to know each other? Can we just surrender to the fact that you don't know what you're doing, I don't know what you're doing, and I don't know what I am doing! So, let's just see what happens when we are here, present and heart-to-heart.'

Having gratitude for where you are now is the first step to creating something incredible because you are creating from a place where you know how much you are already receiving, and the more you are noticing what you are receiving, the fuller your cup. From this place, your cup starts to overflow and when you're in overflow, it's easier to create. It's easier to give because you are overflowing. You are overflowing with love and abundance from what you are receiving, simply by being alive, simply by having the tiniest little things in your life that we just don't notice anymore.

We often take much for granted. We forget what we have already received and that we have many things which other people in the world are dreaming of. We stop noticing. When we start to have a sense of gratitude, we start noticing and get to play from this place. We can be grateful for the fact that we were pregnant and now our baby is safely here. Even if your baby is not sleeping through the night, or your baby has colic, this too shall pass, and you can feel gratitude. You are alive and you baby is here with you. Because most cultures don't celebrate this sacred act fully, it's easy to forget what a miracle this is.

It's incredible when we actually stop and notice these things and don't just unconsciously go through the process of raising a child. If we are not mindful, life can go like this: I was pregnant, then I had a baby, and then I was a mum, and then my baby became a toddler, and then she went to preschool, then I had a teenager, then my babies had babies, and then I died. Life speeds up when we don't notice and are always thinking about where we are going in the future instead of paying attention to the present. Gratitude for what we are receiving now is the vibration that allows us to have the confidence to receive more because we realise we are already and always receiving.

The best bit: As we receive, we give. That is the law of the universe. Love creates love. The more noticing, the more celebration, the more gratitude, the more awareness you have of all of the beautiful things you're receiving in your life, the more you are able to give and express yourself because you feel the safety of being held in abundance, and the more you can accept that much is out of your control, and that trying to control things comes from the mind rather than the heart.

So, the practice for today is how can you cultivate a sense of gratitude? *Notice everything around me with love, how far I've come and who I've become*

Can you write a big, long list of things that you are receiving right now? A big, long list of things that you are abundantly receiving, that you are grateful for. *Breath, food, Esme, Hugo, Tim, family, friends, interactions throughout the day, my body, nature, water, plants, sun, laughter, wisdom, home, cacao*

Can you celebrate those things? *Yoga. business yes,*

Take a moment to breathe in the miracle of your life and of your baby's life as a place to begin this journey of creation.

31

Contemplation Three - Vision

What is the vision for your life? What is it that you desire? What is your intention? What is your legacy to leave on this planet? What are you here to do?

We can forget that we are all here for a reason, that there is something we are here to do. I believe every single person has a soul mission. We are all here to do something very specific that no other person could ever do. Your presence here on the earth is very important and what you do is so valuable. Creating your vision is all about using your imagination and being wildly available for your dreams, and knowing that everything is possible. If you just look around the space that you're in right now, every single thing that you can see around you was once in somebody's imagination, was once dreamt up by somebody. Whether it's a book, a piece of furniture, a piece of flooring, the curtains on the wall, a car, a fence; anything you can see, somebody had an idea that they were going to do that and that was their vision. Then they did it. They executed it. They took action, and it happened. Every single thing around you was once living in someone's imagination. Everything is an act of creation. Everything. When you go and order a sandwich at a local cafe, it's an act of creation. Someone thought, I'm going to make a sandwich and

I'm going to put it together and I'm going to buy these ingredients and I'm going to put it together exactly like this. That sandwich is going to taste different to any other sandwich on the planet. There is no other sandwich like that sandwich. It's been made, especially for you. And when it's in your belly, it's gone, but it's an act of creation.

It is a vision whether it's a sandwich or whether it is a six-figure business. It doesn't matter, the concept is the same. What is it that you want to do and how is it a gift to the world? The sandwich is a gift to the world, the table is a gift to the world, this beautiful candle in front of me now as I write to you, that smells divine, is a gift to the world. Every single thing that I've handpicked to bring into my life has come out of someone's imagination to bring me joy, bring me pleasure. It's all the same vibration. Somebody decided to create something because it brought them joy and because they wanted to bring you joy. And so, your vision for you, for your life and how you want to reinvent yourself, is about your joy and sharing that joy with somebody else in the world. That vision could be the smallest thing. It could be making a cup of tea for your loved one in the morning that brings you joy, or it could be having a charity that you know is protecting the earth, or it could be a million-dollar business, or painting your deepest dreams. It doesn't matter what it is. There's no hierarchy determining which is a greater vision than another. There is no one person who is better than anybody else. We all have access to the same field of imagination and potentiality. We might not all be born with the same resources, and social inequity and injustice exists (I am not spirituality bypassing here or white washing), but we all have access to the infinite wisdom of the universe and the field of creativity. Everybody who can imagine has that access. The difference is that some people imagine and they take action, and some people imagine and they don't take action.

The fun starts when you begin to dream *and* take action. Are you one of the people that believes in the power of dreams, that believes in the magic and believes in creation? Or are you being carried in somebody else's dream and story? Do you want to be creating your own pathway and dream, inviting the characters and the players into your story that bring you joy? You are the author of your story. You get to write the chapters and you get to set the location and create the narrative. When you choose to become the main actor in your story, through your imagination, your desires, your intentions and your aligned actions, and your habits and behaviours, you create your ideal reality. That is how you create your life here. I believe this is the power of every single human being that is on this earth.

Many of us forget how amazing we are but often when you have a baby, this is the moment where you get woken up. You realise your body is a magical portal for life. You grew a human being in your body. If you want any evidence of how powerful and amazing you are as a mother, just look at your baby. That's all you need to do.

For me, my vision started when I went to a baby massage class with Emily. I went because she had very bad colic, which I didn't know was even a thing before I had her. It was a bit of a shock to the system because she was a very unsettled baby. I thought it was all my fault and I thought I was doing something terribly wrong. So, I ended up at a baby massage class. I had to travel a long way to get there, I didn't know where I was, and I didn't know anybody. Back then baby massage was a bit out there and I didn't even know what I was doing there, to be honest; it was kind of a desperate attempt to help Emily with her colic. But this one class changed my life. I was weird, but I felt something spark in my heart and soul, and found myself thinking, wow, there's something really powerful about this, about connection, touch, community, and people coming together, stripping out all of the mind stuff and just being here now. By the time I'd left that one hour class, I had pretty much decided that I was going to leave my career as a lawyer and become a baby massage teacher. This was a radical decision as back then there was no internet, and no smartphones. We had a rackety old computer and dial up connection. It was hard to find a training course; there weren't many and they were all in person. I managed to find one and before I knew it, I was on the course. Then it got weirder. As I was sitting in the four-day course with the IAIM I started thinking, this is really weird. I feel like I'm going to end up training people to teach baby massage and the power of love. At this point I'd gone to one baby massage class, gone to the live training course and had now decided I was going to have my own training school one day. Then a teacher who I had done a pregnancy massage course with, who had an interest in traditional Indian baby massage, approached me and said, 'Can we share the traditional way of baby massage and can you teach for me, and combine it with more about anatomy and physiology?' I said yes. I also knew I wanted to add more on space holding, professionalism, and business from my corporate background, so we threw all those ingredients in the mix and before I knew it, I was starting to work at his college teaching baby massage. I stayed there for a few years, and I had my boys, but I still had this feeling that there was something bigger I was meant to be doing. I felt like I was always going to be teaching lots and lots of people.

When Caspar was about three, I decided to leave the college where I was teaching to start Blossom & Berry.

There was not much to help me get started. There were very limited looking websites, no smartphones, or social media. So, I thought, I'm going to teach people by teaching them via distance learning. I'm going to send out ring binders in the post. I'm going to burn DVDs to help people learn and then people will send me their work to mark in the post. I will mark them and send them back. I thought, I can do this because although I've got my kids and they are under five, I think I can do this by marking in the evenings. I'm going to do my baby massage classes in the day, and this is going to work for me because I know lots of people want to study to teach baby massage, but they haven't got the time to go and train because they're at home with their kids. I figured it would be more convenient for them to study at home. I knew I could record videos (which would mean that I would be 100% certain that students would be able to learn from me), and I felt really passionate about doing this. So, I recorded all the videos on this really rubbish camera; it was pretty basic. I think I had about three people in the first year, and then I had about six people. Year on year the business started to grow, and as it grew so did my excitement. As my children grew, I had more space to balance babies and business. I was able to do both and feel fulfilled. My babies and my business grew at the perfectly aligned rate, which meant that I could be present with both of them.

If my business had grown super-fast, like a rocket at the beginning, I wouldn't have had time to spend with my kids, which was the exact reason why I left my corporate career, so I could be with them. It would have been completely pointless to have left my corporate career just to have an overwhelming entrepreneurial business that sucked all of my time and energy. Every step was perfect; every step, even though it was slow at the start, was meant to be slow because in every step I was learning something. The pace meant I had time to learn all aspects of running and growing my business. I didn't have any experience to begin with. I started off with no money, little time, three children under three and a half, and no idea about being an entrepreneur. There were so many challenges. Sitting at my desk until two o'clock in the morning trying to work out how to design a logo. Trying to work out how do I make a baby massage mat? How do I get labels printed for bottles? How do I burn DVDs? I was doing everything myself back then. I had a whole aromatherapy range that I was blending myself, I had products I was sending out, I had an online shop. I had even designed my own baby massage mat, which back then was impossible to get printed so my best friend was making them up for me at night after her kids went to bed, on her sewing machines, and we were selling them over email. There were so many things I was doing. I was planning, I was creating, and I was refining constantly.

Then eventually the most beautiful things started to happen which I could never have planned. There were so many twists and turns in the story. I started to go global. A beautiful person called Christina from Italy, appeared in my email and said, "I'm a cranial osteopath. Would you train me to become a baby massage instructor? Then I will become your teacher in Italy." I said yes to her, and I flew to Italy to do a teacher training with her in Italian, having never met her before, having not seen anything that she'd translated in terms of my materials, but just trusting that everything would be fine. I got off the plane and I met her in the airport and she said, "We are going to start the training in half an hour." We had never spoken to each other before! We had never had a conversation about how the training was actually going to flow. I showed up at the two-day training with no idea what to expect and it was the most easy, incredible training ever! Christina was translating to me and for me in real time as I don't speak Italian. It was crazy! I couldn't believe I was there, how it had all happened, and how beautiful the whole experience was. It gave me so much faith, trust and confidence in myself and what I was sharing. That was the first major international training I did, and I then went on to do many others in Dubai, Australia, Mexico, Botswana, and Ireland.

It was also Christina that gifted me 'Love Creates Love' which is Blossom & Berry's mantra. On the wall in her studio, there was a circle that said, 'Love creates Love'. As soon as I saw it, it felt like a deep remembrance. I said to Christina, "Would you mind if I shared this concept? It deeply resonates with me because I really feel this is what we are doing at Blossom & Berry, we are creating love. We create love for parents in our circles, parents create love for their babies, babies grow with love and create love for others. This is how we love the world forward, one human being at a time."

I went home from that training, and I completely reorientated Blossom & Berry to the highest vision of love, and it grew and welcomed in so many new teachers. Then other incredible people came into my life. Sandy became my business partner in Mexico, teaching Mexican teachers, and I went over to Mexico with her and taught in Mexico City. Then Mel and Amy came into my life and I flew to Byron Bay and taught teachers in Australia. This then gave me the confidence to offer free training in Malawi to give back to vulnerable parents and babies and to teach in orphanages. That led to me setting up the mother and baby infant health projects in Malawi with Love Support Unite. So can you see how through being in the vibration of love, through being in the vibration of trusting the magic, by holding the vision that I'm here to do great things, that I'm here to serve parents and babies, that I'm here to create connection and community and contribution, beautiful miracles happened. I don't exactly know how they happened, but I believe it was by holding that vibration, holding that desire and holding the excitement, the open-mindedness and the receptivity to receive the people, places and things that would activate the vision. I believe this is the reason that all kinds of incredible, magical things that have happened in my life.

I feel like the luckiest girl alive. I've travelled the world. I've done things I could never, ever dream that I could have done whilst being with my family and being a mother. I have been authentic as a mother. I am the mother that chose to be at home, to read bedtime stories, play tea parties and go on adventures, and I have been the mother that travels, the mother that inspires, the mother that's the leader, the mother that's the visionary. I've been able to take my children to Malawi to see what has been created. My children have come to my events. They have put oil in my bottles for Blossom & Berry. They've been part of the process of my growth, and I have been a part of theirs. They have gained from me being truly me, and I've gained from them being them. As young adults, they all have that free spirit, that open-mindedness, that lack of fear of the world. They are amazing travellers and they're on their own path now.

All of that has come from me holding the vision for myself, from writing the love story of my life, from being open to the magic and mystery, and having the desire and the knowing that this is what it is I'm here to do. Sometimes when I've tried to do other things, the universe just brings me right back so that I don't forget that I'm here to support parents and babies. I'm here to mother mothers. I'm here to protect babies' hearts. I'm here to put family first. I'm here to create love, because love creates love. The universe won't let me forget that. When things haven't worked out, I've been in acceptance about it and known that's not what I'm supposed to do. I trust and I return. I desire to be led by my soul and my heart and to not be led by my head.

So, the invitation for today is:

What is the highest vision for you? work im passionate about, lots of ffs, £3k pm, work life balance, amazing relationship, dream home, travel.

What is the masterpiece of your life? work I love that earns me a £3k+ income pm. Living in my forever home making memories with my family.

What is the love legacy that you want to leave? We are born whole and deserve to live life feeling whole exact as we are.

What is the inspiration that you want to give your children?

As above, no matter what life throws at you you are uniquely amazing and can create the life you want.

What does the love story of your life sound like, feel like? Sounds like a river flowing, wind in the trees, birds singing, sun and rain on my face. Always strong

What happens in it? but equally beautiful I fall so deeply in love with my self that I can accept

Write down some of the headings of the chapters. Remember, you are the creator. Remember, you get to decide because either you decide, or someone decides for you. You either choose or someone chooses for you. This is such an important part of being a mother, being a leader, being an inspiration, setting the vibration for yourself and your family in the world.

Be that light that shines so bright that others see you and think, wow, look at her, look at what she's doing, I can do that too. That is such a gift to your family. There's so much happiness and joy and freedom in the self-expression that comes from creating the vision.

Allow yourself to enter the field of potentiality, the field of imagination and dream big. It's there for every single person. So, allow yourself to connect with that infinite place of possibility and to receive and to remember.

+ love others for who they are we build a life based on joy, acceptance, growth and unconditional love. The everyday little moments are what make the masterpiece of our life.

43

Contemplation Four - Planning

Planning is something that I love, but maybe not in the way that you imagine. I am a very spontaneous person, I take big leaps, I am a YES person, I love to have flow, *but* I also love to plan. A plan is very different to having goals. A lot of people have goals: what they want to achieve, a certain level of fitness, weight, a certain income goal, etc. The issue with goals is that we can become attached to them. We can hold them tightly and view our success in terms of whether we have achieved them or not. A plan is different. A plan is spacious and expansive. A plan has creativity built into it. A plan has flexibility, A plan has room for magic and all of the possible things that can come in. When you have a plan, it feels like an intention for the future. With a plan there is room to rearrange and to know that aspects can move backwards and forwards. You know that the plan can alter. You know that people, places and things can come in so you can hold it lightly. This creates expansiveness. It creates a vibration of limitlessness. It creates a vibration of curiosity and playfulness, and it creates a vibration of co-creation with the universe.

Something that I've always done is have a diary. I only use the monthly planner and I don't put in my diary day-to-day goals as such. Obviously, I have appointments and things like that but when I look at my diary I think, what is the vibration of September? What is it that I want to achieve in September? What is the theme of September? Am I feeling sociable? Do I feel like I want to travel? Am I feeling like I really want to finish this book or write this course? Am I feeling like I need to be present with my kids? Is it someone's birthday? So, I put things I want to bring into my energetic field that month, and then I feel into it, and plan. I ask myself, in order to do that, what do I need to do? Let's work backwards and reverse engineer what I need to do in order to achieve this? In this way you are not stuck with rigid goals. If you get up one day and you feel not in the mood to do something you don't do it, as there is something else that feels more alive to you. You can have flexibility as you know there is room within the plan. So, if you have a desire to write a course in September but now is not the moment, move it to January. Instant stress gone! You're back in the game. You're back in the flow. You're back in creativity. You're back honouring your energy. One thing that I've learned from being a dynamic creator for twenty years is that you are always pregnant with some kind of idea. We don't know how long the pregnancy is going to be. We don't know when the idea will be born. You know, I've been pregnant with some ideas for like four years! My Nurturing The Future Event that I created for over eighty people in London was in my field for years. I didn't know exactly when it would come or how but when it did, it was amazing! I kept moving the timeline because, first of all there was COVID, but also, I just wasn't ready. I don't know how I knew, but there was something that needed to happen for me before I was ready. Things needed to happen. I was just allowing time and experience to come into my field so that I was the best version of me at the point when it happened. And then one day, I just knew I was ready. And I made it happen.

This is the juiciness of spacious creation, of expansive creation where you are just allowing yourself to be, and you are not forcing yourself to do anything before you are ready. You are making a commitment to yourself that this is what you desire to birth in the future. Some days you are going to be more in the vibration and identity of the person that matches your dream, and some days you are not. And that's okay because we don't have to be consistent. We are not robots. We have feelings and life happens and things come up, which means that we need to have this flexibility so that we don't throw the baby out with the bath water and say, because this didn't happen today, it will never happen. You can flip it over to the next month or flip it over to the next year. You stay in the intention and make small moves towards what you desire and allow yourself the kindness and compassion to change. Babies don't walk in a day; they don't even have to practice walking every day in order to get there. They get there eventually through opportunity, curiosity, and courage to try something new and get back up when they fall.

I have got so many ideas at the moment written in my journal for what it is that I desire. And I absolutely know 100% that I'm going to do those but to be honest, there is about five years' worth of work there. I'm excited about the next five years because I've got intentions for each one of those years. I've got a reason to get excited. I've got a passion and a purpose. In between all those things happening, I absolutely know that beautiful things are going to drop into my field. Some of those things might drop off again, some of them might come back, some of them might turn into ten-year projects, or twenty-year projects. Some of them aren't meant to be. That's all okay because you are honouring what's alive in you now.

Here are a few stories of going with the flow that embody what I believe. I went on holiday with my kids to Sorrento a couple of years ago and I was actually feeling a little bit broken-hearted because I was dating a guy and it hadn't worked out. One morning I went off and I was sitting having this beautiful coffee in this amazing Italian harbour in Sorrento feeling so lucky, so blessed, and I got out my journal and I started to write poetry. I wrote Magic Love Spells for Babies (one of my now published books), which is a whole series of beautiful poems that you can read to your baby or to yourself. They are all about honouring the magic of babies through our words. It was such a beautiful book. The poems and the words just flowed through me. I didn't have to do anything; I just opened my journal. I was just writing and writing and writing. When I came back to the UK I got the poems, made a book cover on Canva, and within two weeks I'd published that book. I've had numerous things like this happen to me. I have another book called 'I Am Love' (a Children's book), which I wrote when my children went to see their dad on Boxing Day just after I was divorced. It was a really painful day and so I opened my laptop and, for some reason that I do not know, I had this book come through me. I know that it's not me writing these books, it's not Gayle Berry, the human that does it, it's the essence of me. It's what wants to come through me. So, on that day when I was in a lot of pain, I got right out of my way, and I ended up writing this book on a Boxing Day afternoon by myself. By the time the kids had come home, it was done. I published it within a month. It just wanted to come through me. It might surprise you that this book came through me in four hours on a Sunday night with no notice, but I was just ready and open to receiving the words and turning them into a book. That's what happens when I release goals and allow things to flow. Humans like goals because we like to tick things off and tell ourselves, 'I've done that. That was good, I'm a success.' But there will always be another goal. There's so much more that can come into your reality that you can't even think of. There's so much that you can receive that you can't even dream of, when you hold it lightly. That is how I have run my business for over twenty years, and I'm still in love with it. Yes, I've had challenging experiences, but I'm still in love with it. I'm still so grateful for it and it still flows through me, and I still am so blessed, and I never want it to end. I want that flow to stay with me.

The invitation for today is what is the loose plan?

£3K+ pm, doing work I love, good work life balance, Huge happy.

What is the expansive plan?

Grow the business so lots of business flows to me, can earn passive income.

What are the things that you would love to do this year?

Go self employed fully.
Earn £3K pm +
Successful classes + circles.

What are the things you'd like to do in five years' time?

Reach and help more people globally!
Give to charity.
Sell online for passive income

What are the things you'd like to do in ten years' time?

49

What are the things that you would love to be able to share? It could be holidays, or going to a place that you've never been before, taking a training, or having dinner in a beautiful restaurant. It could be making a charitable donation, volunteering for something, or redecorating your house. What are the things that hold this beautiful vibration of joy and pleasure for yourself and others, and for the world?

I'd love for you to have a little plan and then you can let me know how you get on. Have fun with this and remember to tap into your imagination and trust that everything is possible.

Contemplation Five - Action

Now it's time for action: how to take action, how to not burn out and how not to be depleted, especially when you are balancing motherhood and business.

I can honestly say, I've never burnt out in the last twenty-two years. I've actually had a little bit of a tricky time in the last six months because I've been going through the menopause, which is definitely another moment of reinvention. I've had a lot of grief for ending this mother phase of my life in terms of my energetic ability to create through my womb, through my menstrual cycle. It's been a wild ride and I've had so much gratitude for every single moment that I've spent with my kids, which is part of the reason why I am sharing this book with you now. My advice to you is stay present, stay connected, celebrate the hell out of everything with your children. Have deep gratitude for everything NOW. Stay in the moment and just say thank you every single day for everything that you are receiving, because it is a gift.

Taking aligned action in the now is really important. For me, actions should feel like flow; you want to feel like water. Water can flow quickly, it can flow slowly, it can flow over bumpy rocks that splash it around, it can go over waterfalls, but it still keeps flowing. As it flows, it changes shape, and it moves. That is how I desire you to take action in your life and in your business. I want you to flow. When you go with the flow, it just feels effortless and easy. The way to create flow is first of all to look after yourself, to optimise your health. You've got to eat well, you've got to rest, you've got to look after yourself. You've got to put yourself first. You've got one job on this planet and that's to look after you. Nobody is going to look after you like you can look after you. You are the main character in your story, and you get to choose how to look after yourself. It's nobody's fault if you are not cared for as that's your primary job! If you need help and support, you must ask. You must honour your needs above everything else. This can be so hard as a mother, but I promise you that you are gifting your children with this ability when you do it for yourself. We have to let go of all of the judgments, the expectations, the beliefs, the stories, or the thoughts of anyone around us, and honour ourselves. You can only create what you desire when you know yourself, what you need and want, and when you have connected to the essence of you. You must be authentic to the version of you that exists now, so you don't have to put any effort into being anything other than who you are. You're just you and you are going to allow yourself to be fully expressed. Be honest with yourself and others. It's going to save you so much stress and anxiety and energy in the long run.

You've got to be devoted to you and what you desire. You are a unique expression of love and light. You are never going to be repeated and it's a miracle you are here. The seed of love and light within you is perfect. You've got to stay with your programme, so when you take action it comes from the most optimised version of you. You've got to love yourself to take action. Allow all of you and allow yourself to be seen.

With your actions, you want them to be in balance and harmony between the two vibrations of masculine and feminine energies. Both exist in us regardless of our gender. The masculine energy is the doing, it's the passion and the purpose. It's more of the linear push energy. It's the energy that gets things done in life. It's the energy of the to-do list. It's the energy of the jobs. It's the energy of the practicality. The feminine energy is the energy of creativity, of abundance, believing, knowing, dreaming. It's the energy of the magic, of the serendipity, of all of the things that you can't possibly imagine that can come into existence as the great creator. Think of the frequency of Mother Earth, fully abundant and providing for us. Creating all of the time, caring for all expressions of life. That is the vibration of the feminine.

When taking action, we need to be in both these vibrations. We need to have the feminine knowing that we are connected to the vision, the imagination, the creation, the magic, the possibility of anything happening, *with* the masculine energy of the doing, the consistency and the safety of taking purposeful steps to the destination.

It's the being and the doing coming into harmony with each other that creates this flow in life. It means that when you're making decisions, they are coming from a place where you're not burnt out and you are also not afraid. The masculine energy of doing gives you safety because the more you do, the more evidence you have in reality that the thoughts and beliefs that you are holding in the feminine energy of the potentiality and creativity, are going to come into reality because the masculine energy is paving the way. The masculine energy is the frequency that goes out looking for something to eat, to hunt, and comes back with what is needed. The feminine energy is the energy that receives it, celebrates it, makes it taste delicious and makes it feel amazing. Both energies are there to learn and grow intuitively. When those energies are in balance that is what creates inspired action. When you're taking inspired and aligned action, you'll know how it feels in your body. If what you're doing is depleting you, burning you out, causing you physical pain in your body, keeping you awake at night, you need to notice and choose a different way.

You create amazing things when your masculine and feminine energy come together. It also creates excitement and polarity within yourself. You can feel empowered that you went out and did it. Then you can sit back and really enjoy it because your masculine energy created this for you. You can really receive it.

It's a really lovely feeling to experience. It's a beautiful vibration within your body. The feminine is also there to celebrate the masculine going out and 'doing'. This is why celebration is so important. If you are always doing and you're never celebrating, then there's no point in 'doing' because you're just 'doing for the sake of doing' and accumulating and getting more and more goals and more things. The feminine energy helps you to cherish and love what you have now and to stop, be, celebrate, and enjoy, and to be in that beautiful vibration of abundance.

I believe life comes through you and you are this beautiful channel for this soul purpose that you are here to share with others. I believe, whether it's a little smile or creating a new way that changes the lives of billions of people, that everything we do is to be of service, to be connecting, to help other people. There's no other reason to be here other than that and to enjoy it and grow through challenges.

So, the invitation is to feel into the following:

Are you in your masculine or feminine energy most of the time? *At the moment more feminine, used to be more masculine.*

How much are you doing and how much are you being yourself? *I feel I am being myself more in my classes.*

How much are you really celebrating yourself? *Not enough.*

How much are you really allowing yourself to receive that abundance? *I believe I have belief blocking it. NB- I am abundant from*

How much are you sharing your energy with others and creating nurturing, beautiful experiences from it? *Not enough.*

What things in your life make you feel good? *Helping others see how amazing they are.*

What things do you either need to stop doing, delegate, or learn how to do better so they don't feel as hard, so you can do them?

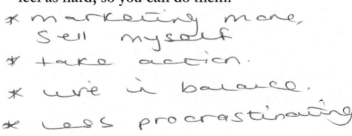

* marketing more, sell myself
* take action.
* live in balance.
* less procrastinating

A Closing Word…

I hope you feel inspired by this transmission. I hope you feel like you are the magical human being that you are. I hope you remember who you are in your essence: a beautiful expression of love. You are a sacred one in a million miracle of life here to do great things.

Becoming a mother is not the end. It's the beginning because it's the waking up to the realisation that you are the greatest creator that there has ever been in this version of you. You nurtured a human life. Now you get to be a leader. You get to be the ancestor that your future generations will be proud of. You get to heal intergenerational trauma through kindness and compassion. You get to create a new vibration for your family. You get to do all of these things and you get to have so much fun and pleasure in doing it.

Yes, there are going be challenges. I'm not going to sugarcoat it, but that's all part of the experience. That's all part of the lessons you get to learn, and sometimes in those lessons there is gold. It's a journey. It's co-creation. It's a miracle. It's magic. It's incredible. Have so much gratitude for it all. We don't have any control, we are in surrender, and accepting that is so important. It's an illusion that we can control; we can only accept and be love.

You are creating the vibration for your family. You are the soil in which the seed was planted and continues to grow. You can choose how to nourish and nurture yourself, what to do and what to be. When we all realise how powerful we are, we get a chance to change the world into a more connected and loving place. It's safe to reinvent yourself, it's safe to let go. It's safe to let yourself be born again into another version of you. Choose to live life fully and freely, and all will align. Believe in your magic as a mother and know you are incredible. I see you and I believe in you.

Much love

Gayle

To find out more about my projects you can visit:

www.blossomandberry.com

www.iamgayleberry.com

www.villagevisionary.co.uk

www.lovesupportunite.org

www.lovespecs.org

Thank you every person who has seen me, heard me, supported me and loved me on my journey. I am grateful for you all.

Love creates love

Monday.
Am yoga,
business planning
pm

Tuesday.   9.30 - 3.30   6hrs.
Sian full day. 50/50
Wednesday.   6hrs.
~~Sian~~ class 12-1pm   50/50
Sian work 2.15 - 8pm
       (could Tim be around).
                    12 hours

Thurs + friday.
new place.   16hours.

Every other Saturday
      9 - 2pm   5 hours.

            Ave
       week 1 - 28 hrs.
       week 2 - 33 hrs.
            + classes.

Benefits for Sian

- Doesn't have to pay me when I'm not busy.
- Incentivises me to fill diary.
- I'm not included in her tax so she can earn more.
- Sian can use room Thursdays.

* Check Winnington can do earlier weds.
* Tim Hugo.
* Daycare Thurs/friday.
* circles once month monday eve?
* Do price list, what do I want to do?
    - Business aim.
    - MN etc)
    - Botanicals?
    - Simone treatments?
    - Sports to go and advertise as time.
    - Reiki, sound bowls. Meditation,

* Support a charity
* Business vision.

Printed in Great Britain
by Amazon

28652567R10036